Becoming a Woman of Worth:

Creating a More Confident You

KRISTEN CLARK

READER COMMENTS

"Kristen Clark's book, Becoming A Woman of Worth, walks us through our analysis of who we are, who we could be, and how to attain this… I highly recommend Kristen's book, whether you're just interested in self-reflection or if you have problems with your self-esteem. This book will give you guidance in your journey."

Gloria Penwell, new-author mentor, writer's conference assistant director, and representative of AMG Publishers

"Though I am a man, my experience as a residential treatment counselor for adolescent women drew me to this book. Becoming a Woman of Worth was and is exactly what many of the young ladies that I have worked with needed to have in their hands and in their hearts. Kristen Clark gives true, practical suggestions, many of which we used in our program, but she goes a step further and shows how God blesses rather than frowns upon building our self-worth. The truth of what Kristen has written applies not only to women, but to everyone."

Bil Howard for Readers' Favorite

"I wish Becoming a Woman of Worth had been available when I was facing divorce after 18 years of marriage. I have since come to realize I was in textbook depression with a non-existent self-worth. While reading the book, I often nodded my head in agreement with the author."

Barbara Arent, Romance-Suspense Author

"Ms. Clark takes the reader along a journey that enables each one to better understand how they can become that person of worth and value. There are detailed bits of information given that will show a person what to do, how to do it, and the results that one should expect by making these life-changing choices... This is a very encouraging book and one that will help to improve one's life if read with an open and willing heart."

Darin Godby for Readers' Favorite

BECOMING A WOMAN OF WORTH

KRISTEN CLARK

American Mutt Press

Copyright © 2014 Kristen Clark

Cover Photograph by Kristen Clark

All rights reserved.

ISBN: 0976459132
ISBN-13: 978-0976459132

DEDICATION

To those who have gone before me in becoming a Woman of Worth, and who have helped me do the same by learning to see myself as God sees me: my cup runneth over with joy and gratitude.

To my husband, for your endless encouragement and applause of the woman I am today and the woman I aspire to be. I love you dearly.

CONTENTS

A Few Introductory Words

Part I: Reflections on Confidence and Self-Esteem

How Precious Are Your Thoughts About Yourself?	19
How Confidence Helps Me Prevail	23
The Difference Between Confidence and Arrogance	27
Three Reasons Why Confidence is the Key to Success	31
Myths About Self-Esteem	33
Mistakes People Make When Building Confidence	37

Part II: Practical Suggestions for Building Confidence

HALT! And Rise Above Feelings of Inferiority	41
Journal Through Your Emotions	43

Instill Confidence Through Letter Writing	47
Give Yourself Permission	49
Change What You Can, Pray About What You Can't	53
Learn Something New	57
Use Your Creativity	59
Share Your Expertise	63
Speak Up for Yourself	67
Discover and Celebrate Hidden Talents	71
Overcome Anxiety in Social Situations	75
Practice the Three P's of Confidence	79
Learn to Accept Compliments	83
Set Clearly Defined Goals	85
Maintain a Confident Mindset for Greater Personal Success	89
Reduce Stress Through the Holidays	93

Part III: An Exploration of Confidence as a Spiritual Mindset

Convictions and the Road to Confidence	99
Two Steps Forward and One Giant Step Back	103
Loneliness and Practical Steps for Overcoming It	105
The Truth About Emotional Healing	107
Healing from Abuse: Regaining Self Value and Worth in the Wake of God's Love	113
Six Ways to Grow Spiritually, Connect with God, and Increase Confidence	117
Fear-Conquering Scripture	121
Esteem-Building Scripture	127
Bible Study Tips	131
Woman of Worth Affirmation	135
How You Can Help	137

About the Author

A FEW INTRODUCTORY WORDS

How do you feel about yourself most days? Do you feel confident, self-assured, empowered, and ready to tackle the world? Or do you feel less than, undeserving, ill-equipped, and insufficient?

How we feel about ourselves plays a critical role in our overall success, and negative feelings can cause us to sell ourselves short and impede our ability to reach our highest potential. We may say things or act in ways that suggest we are anything short of capable and effective, which can lead to:

- Quickly dismissing compliments
- Feeling like we have nothing to contribute or offer
- Allowing others to seize opportunities ahead of us
- Worrying about what others will think of us
- Procrastinating as a result of fear of failure

These negative feelings can vary from woman to woman in terms of degree. Some women have small battles with this, while others are consumed and incapacitated by this emotional state. And yet, this just isn't something we talk about in public. I don't personally hear discussions that are designed to address this subject. Do you?

Wouldn't you like to:

- Celebrate compliments with grace and gratitude?
- Use your God-given gifts and talents to participate and contribute?
- Seize opportunities for yourself, as God presents them?
- Embrace your divine worth and value so the approval of others will no longer be essential?
- Move forward in confidence and overcome obstacles?

Thankfully, there is a solution. We can begin to see our value and become Women of Worth:

- By looking in toward our natural and learned abilities and personal experiences, and
- By looking up toward our Heavenly Father for our role and value in His Kingdom.

By looking in and looking up we can embrace our character assets and align our thoughts about ourselves with how God thinks about us. We can grow in confidence and reach higher levels of personal success.

This book is a compliment to my 21 Day Journey, an online program designed to help women develop the daily habit of finding their value in the scriptures in an effort to build the confidence needed to fulfill their noble purpose – that's the "looking up." For more information on this program, please visit:

http://hissideofthelookingglass.com/introductory-offer/

I hope you enjoy this book and find it empowering in your effort to embrace your natural and learned abilities and personal experiences – that's the "looking in."
You are a Woman of Worth and this is your opportunity to create a more confident you. Enjoy the adventure!

Cheers!

KRISTEN CLARK

PART I
REFLECTIONS ON CONFIDENCE AND SELF-ESTEEM

KRISTEN CLARK

HOW PRECIOUS ARE YOUR THOUGHTS ABOUT YOURSELF?

One of my favorite scriptures is Psalm 139, which beautifully describes God's love for us. In fact, Bible teachers agree that of all the Psalms this one best illustrates God's personal relationship with us; it reminds us that God sees everything about us, is constantly with us, created a plan for us, and is continually leading us to fulfill His plan.

I think all of this is best summed up in two short verses, Psalm 139:17-18: *"How precious are your thoughts about me, O God. They cannot be numbered! I can't even count them; they outnumber the grains of sand!"*

These two verses are short and sweet, but pose a few challenging questions.

- How can God think so highly of us?
- Are our thoughts about ourselves equally precious?
- As children of the Most High King, why do we say things or behave in ways that suggest we are anything short of dearly loved, divinely blessed, and created for a noble purpose?

The answer to these questions can be found in 1 Corinthians 13:12, which reminds us that we are looking in a mirror that gives only a dim or blurred reflection; our self-reflection (or self-image) is smudged or distorted. This can lead to:

- Quickly dismissing compliments
- Feeling like we have nothing to contribute or offer
- Allowing others to seize opportunities ahead of us
- Worrying about what others will think of us

Thankfully, life is a journey of progress and not perfection, and **we can improve our blurred reflection by taking up the Sword of the Spirit.** We can find a healthy dose of just how much God loves us in the Bible and start to have as much respect for ourselves as God has for us. Wouldn't you like to:

- Celebrate compliments with grace and gratitude?
- Use your God-given gifts and talents to participate and contribute?
- Seize opportunities for yourself, as God presents them?
- Embrace your divine worth and value so the approval of others will no longer be essential?

In essence, by looking to the scriptures to understand how precious God's thoughts are of us, we can begin to see ourselves with increased clarity and confidence.

Which scripture verses should we start with? I suggest starting with the scriptures verses on page 121 in this book. Read those verses and pray them for yourself. Read what your study Bible says about them and take them to heart for it is within these verses you will discover the most incredible treasure. It is within these verses you will discover YOU!

KRISTEN CLARK

HOW CONFIDENCE HELPS ME PREVAIL

As a woman wearing many hats, I have learned the value of confidence. It is only with this assurance I am able to triumphantly meet the needs of my employer, serve my husband and family, and shepherd others in ministry. However, having confidence didn't come naturally. I developed it through the daily habit of aligning my thoughts about myself with what God says about me.

For me, this exercise needs to be a daily habit; otherwise my mind becomes a playground for the enemy's voice and I begin to feel undeserving, ill-equipped, and insufficient. Simple tasks become significant challenges. I hesitate to:

- volunteer for new projects at the office,
- initiate a creative date night with my husband, or
- forgive harsh criticism from church members.

My best intentions become the target of fear (of failure, rejection, or exposure). I rationalize and justify behavior that contradicts my efforts and I start to question my ability.

Why do I think I can do this or that project? What if my husband thinks my idea is stupid? What grand experience or insights can I offer those in my small group? Why me?

To overcome these negative thoughts, I practice three daily steps:

1. Read scripture each morning.
2. Look up the definitions and synonyms of the key words in verses I have read.
3. Read what my study Bible says about each verse and any referenced scripture.

These easy steps are manageable each morning. A few scripture verses are enough for me to internalize and apply to my situations throughout the day. Looking up key words and synonyms in a dictionary allows me to correct any definitions I had wrong. Reading what my study Bible says about each verse gives me clarity about the verse's context, history, and application.

By following these three steps, I get a daily dose of my value and worth. The question *why me?* then becomes *why NOT me?!*

I am a child of the Most High King. I am His ambassador, set apart for a holy purpose. I have been hand-picked, hand-chosen, and mercifully forgiven. I am the work of His hand. I have been created perfectly and for His glory. AND I can do all things through Him who strengthens me.

The end result? *Feelings* are replaced by *facts*. Confidence returns and I become able to volunteer for that special project at work, plan a fun and creative evening with my husband, or respond to constructive feedback from church members.

Staying immersed in the scriptures helps me avoid having my self-confidence stolen, killed, or destroyed. Thankfully, I have been given authority to overcome the enemy, which I do by wielding the Sword of the Spirit. In this way, I rise above and prevail.

KRISTEN CLARK

THE DIFFERENCE BETWEEN CONFIDENCE AND ARROGANCE

People who long for more confidence and higher levels of self-esteem are often discouraged from seeking a deeper belief in self because they are afraid they will become arrogant. This fear often stems from a misperception about the differences between confidence and arrogance. What is the difference?

There may appear to be a fine line between confidence and arrogance, but really the two couldn't be more different. Confidence *inspires* while arrogance *discourages*. Confidence is *healthy* while arrogance is *destructive*. Confidence is *noble* while arrogance is *annoying*. Read on to explore specific behaviors of confident and arrogant people. Next, ask yourself which one you are.

Arrogance is an exaggerated opinion of one's worth or importance and often comes across as superiority. Ironically, many people who suffer from arrogance are really trying to *hide* their *insecurities*. They tend to *overly compensate* for their *weaknesses*, which results in *pompous self-importance*. Here are some typical behaviors of arrogant people:

- Name dropping out of context
- Using condescending phrases
- Harshly criticizing and judging others
- Strutting or swaggering into a room

- Dominating conversations and discussions
- Appearing to know everything
- Interrupting conversations to be heard
- Having answers for everything
- Bragging and one-upping others
- Blaming others for their mistakes
- Taking credit for all the work

Confidence, on the other hand, is a faith or belief that one will behave in the right, proper, or effective way.

People with confidence *trust* their *instincts* and naturally do what they believe to be *right, appropriate,* and *productive or fruitful.* Here are some typical behaviors of confident people:

- Showing a genuine interest in others
- Encouraging and complimenting others when appropriate and deserved
- Accepting one's weaknesses and lack of skills
- Hearing and benefitting from constructive feedback and criticism
- Bouncing back after setbacks with grace and dignity
- Listening to others with an open mind
- Admitting one's limited knowledge with a willingness to learn from others
- Voicing opinions in love and kindness
- Celebrating the victories of others

- Accepting responsibility and learning from past mistakes
- Giving credit where credit is due

The good news is that confidence can be developed and nurtured, and doesn't have to turn into arrogance. We can all develop a quiet certitude and suffocate an exaggerated sense of pride. In other words, we can choose to see ourselves with clarity, and not more highly than we really are (Romans 12:3), but it starts with a sober assessment of ourselves.

Which are you? Are you consumed with self-importance or do you humbly celebrate an inner trust in yourself, your actions, and your choices? If you decide to seek the latter, don't let the fear of arrogance keep you from achieving your goal. Confidence is a virtue to be celebrated.

THREE REASONS WHY CONFIDENCE IS THE KEY TO SUCCESS

I read a lot of books on how to build a successful business. I've read "how to" books for writers, speakers, life coaches, internet marketers, business strategists, and budding entrepreneurs. The one thing these books all have in common is a chapter on confidence. As Samuel Johnson once said, "Self-confidence is the first requisite to great undertakings."

How we think and feel about ourselves has an enormous impact on our ability to perform. A healthy self-image can tip the scales in our favor and equip us with the grace we need to push forward in victory, even through the most difficult situations. It gives us the mindset we need to prevail; below are three reasons why.

1. Navigate Change. Confidence provides the flexibility we need to look ahead and redirect goals in the midst of changing conditions and environments. It allows us to trust our own ideas, perceptions, and opinions, and gives us courage to voice our feelings and beliefs. It helps us make timely decisions and stretches ourselves as needed. Finally, it gives us a winning history to lean on through times of uncertainty.

2. Overcome Setbacks. Confidence helps us avoid procrastination as a result of perfectionism and gives us the ability to push forward and accomplish difficult tasks. It enables us to accept our weaknesses and lack of skills while hearing and benefitting from constructive feedback and criticism. It empowers us to learn from past mistakes, rather than repeating them. It allows us to develop the persistence and fortitude needed to bounce back from defeat and move forward.

3. Meet the Needs of Others. Confidence provides excellent interpersonal skills and the ability to get along with others. It enables us to be positive, energetic, assertive, and encouraging even among difficult personalities. It increases our ability to think critically, negotiate, and propose solutions for the greater good of the group. It also builds credibility with others and enables a spirit of humility when needed.

Trying times have shown me the value of confidence. With a positive self-image I have successfully transitioned between relationships, jobs, and geographical locations. I have bounced back from workforce reductions and painful job reshuffling. And I have served well my family, clients, and community in spite of opposing personalities. Confidence has allowed me to do all of this and push forward to greater victory.

Having a healthy dose of confidence allows us to take life on life's terms with greater personal success. It gives us a positive belief in our abilities and potential, and significantly affects our effort and performance. When we believe we can, we do – even when it seems all odds are against us.

MYTHS ABOUT SELF-ESTEEM

Don't let commonly held myths interfere with your effort to build self-esteem. If you long to feel confident, self-assured, empowered, and ready to tackle the world, learn the facts about self-esteem and ignore the myths that can hold you back.

Commonly held beliefs are often grounded in long-standing myths lacking any real evidence to support them. Isn't that true of so many things today? For example, feeding a cold and starving a fever is not always the best advice; being sick often kills your appetite so force-feeding isn't necessarily a good idea. A wet head doesn't make you sick, a low immune system does; you might feel chilly with wet hair, but not much else will happen because wet hair doesn't increase susceptibility to infection. Julius Caesar didn't wear a laurel wreath for victory's sake; he wore it for vanity's sake because he was going bald.

Unfortunately, myths like these also exist about self esteem. Did you know that people with low self-esteem aren't always the product of a rough childhood? Even individuals who grew up in ideal environments can still feel insufficient, inferior, and undeserving. Create a more confident you by learning the facts about these dangerous myths.

Myth: People with low self-esteem were battered or abused as children. While this may be true sometimes, it is not always the case. I'm a perfect example. I was raised in a warm and loving family where I received constant words of encouragement and sufficient votes of confidence. However, I developed a low self-image as a result of misperceptions and seeing situations through distorted lenses. Many people suffer from low self esteem because they misinterpret personal wants, needs, prejudices, experiences, education, and memories. The role of their environment or parental engagement often had little to do with it.

Myth: Low self-esteem causes fear. Actually, low self-esteem is the result of fear. People with low self-esteem suffer from one or many fears including fear of doing something that will validate their inadequacy, fear of losing what they have, or fear of never achieving what they want. Fear of abandonment is also a significant contributing factor. Fortunately, feelings are not facts and people can overcome low self-confidence by first conquering their fear.

Myth: People with low self-esteem will never overcome it. Low self-esteem can be overcome with the daily practice of confidence-building exercises. Learning something new, sharing one's expertise with others, and using one's creativity all build confidence. Developing healthy convictions, journaling through negative emotions, and learning to accept compliments also all build confidence. Self-esteem is how someone sees him or herself and can be nurtured just like any other character trait or attitude.

Myth: People with high self-esteem are arrogant. Arrogance is an exaggerated opinion of one's worth or importance and is often displayed as superiority. In fact, many people who suffer from arrogance are really trying to cover their insecurities. Self-esteem, however, is a satisfaction with one's self; a respect and regard for self. People with healthy levels of self-esteem are confident in their abilities and opinions without name-dropping, using condescending phrases, harshly criticizing or judging others, or appearing to know everything. They are comfortable with their strengths and don't need to boast about their accomplishments. They are also comfortable with the weaknesses and can admit when they are wrong.

People turn their lives around every day by learning new behavior and thinking differently about themselves. People lose weight, stop smoking, eat healthier, and expand their knowledge all the time. Developing and maintaining confidence is no different, but desire without knowledge is ineffective (Proverbs 19:2). Don't impede your efforts by believing the myths. The fact is, with intentional effort and discipline, people with deep insecurities can develop higher levels of self-esteem and live happier and more successful lives.

KRISTEN CLARK

MISTAKES PEOPLE MAKE WHEN BUILDING CONFIDENCE

Some people are born confident and self-assured; they seem to know exactly what they want and have little or no reservations about deserving it. Others have a tendency to pass up opportunities because of feelings of inadequacy and inferiority. Thankfully, confidence can be developed. However, it's important to avoid the common mistakes people make in the process.

The good news is that confidence can be developed and nurtured in an effort to achieve higher levels of personal success. With a concentrated and intentional effort, we can all gain the confidence we need to go further – professionally and personally. Start developing higher levels of confidence today and avoid these three common mistakes in the process.

1. Fail to make it a daily habit. Habits are behavior patterns developed from frequent repetition of an activity, and psychiatrists and psychologists agree it takes an average of twenty-one days to break a habit or start a new one. Increase your success of building confidence by making positive thinking about yourself a daily habit. Do something every day to reinforce your value and worth. Learn something new. Share your expertise with someone else. Create something with your mind and hands. Repeat positive affirmations about yourself. Journal about your accomplishments and character assets. If needed, schedule time on your calendar for building and maintaining confidence every day.

2. Fail to identify an accountability partner. Research shows that stating a goal out loud and writing it down increases the chance of reaching that goal. Sharing that goal with another human being makes achieving that goal almost a sure thing. Identify someone to hold you accountable in your effort to develop the habit of daily confidence. Your accountability partner should respect your confidentiality, pass no judgment of your efforts and challenges, and help you stay on target by checking your progress. Knowing someone else is watching your success is a great motivator toward your end result.

3. Fail to celebrate the victories. Our ability to build confidence requires us to identify, acknowledge, and embrace our personal accomplishments. Take time to look at what you have already done. Remind yourself of any obstacles you had to overcome to complete the task. Notice how well you accomplished your goal. Identify the positive attributes that contributed to your accomplishments. Focus on the positive feelings you experienced with your accomplishment. Share your victories with someone you trust and ask for their acknowledgement.

Proverbs 15:12 warns us to embrace correction and seek council. Learn from the mistakes of others. Make the conscious decision to develop the confidence you need to take your desired action. By making your effort a daily habit, getting support from an accountability partner, and celebrating even the smallest of victories, you can develop a positive belief in your abilities and potential. You will quickly begin performing better as a result.

PART II
PRACTICAL SUGGESTIONS FOR BUILDING CONFIDENCE

HALT! AND RISE ABOVE FEELINGS OF INFERIORITY

Feelings come and go. One day we feel like we're on top of the world. The next day we feel like the world is on top of us. Did you know that feelings are also often the result of how well we take care of ourselves?

Our needs are important and making time to care for those needs can contribute to long-term feelings of wellbeing. When we neglect our own needs and forget to nurture ourselves, we run the risk of deeper levels of low self-esteem. When my needs go unmet I can easily become overwhelmed by feelings of inferiority, which cause me to:

- Unfairly criticize myself
- Overreact to the actions and comments of others
- Second-guess myself
- Believe things to be impossible

Thankfully, I discovered a simple method that helps me take care of myself in my effort to maintain confidence through most situations. Often used in addiction recovery, **the HALT method suggests pausing long enough to assess if I am Hungry, Angry, Lonely, or Tired.**

If I am hungry, I make time for a meal or quick snack.

If I am angry, I take a few extra minutes to detach from my stressful situation; I breathe, relax, stretch my limbs, count to ten, pray, and emotionally regroup.

If I am lonely and feeling secluded, I lift my spirits by visiting a neighbor or friend.

If I am tired, I withdraw for a nap and some quiet time in an effort to recharge my battery.

The HALT method allows me to tend to my immediate needs and maintain an attitude of confidence. When I'm strong – physically, mentally, and emotionally – I am more effective because I am free to:

- Take risks by learning from my mistakes rather than repeating them
- Hear and benefit from constructive feedback and criticism
- Trust my own ideas, perceptions, and opinions with the courage to voice my feelings and beliefs
- Hope for and expect success

Proverbs 18:14 reminds us that our spirit can sustain a broken body, but when the spirit dies so does our hope. Using the HALT method, I take care of myself and protect my spirit of confidence so I can move forward in faith.

JOURNAL THROUGH YOUR EMOTIONS

Feelings of self-doubt and inadequacy can be overwhelming; they can draw us into hand-to-hand combat with emotions of hopelessness and helplessness. The good news is feelings are not facts, and psychologists suggest journaling as a useful tool for processing negative feelings and gaining self-awareness by thinking through the facts.

Not only is journaling a safe vehicle for venting and releasing negative emotions that would otherwise be bottled up, it is also a helpful tool for sifting through how we feel during our daily activities. Our minds are often swimming with the busyness of our schedules, and we don't always get the chance to pinpoint why we feel the way we do in any given situation or moment.

Journaling allows us to do just that. It also allows us to get to know ourselves better.

The act of putting feelings into words is also helpful because it lessens their energy and control over us. A brain imaging study by UCLA psychologists revealed why verbalizing our feelings makes our sadness, anger, and pain less intense. Matthew D. Lieberman, UCLA Associate Professor of Psychology and a pioneer of social cognitive neuroscience, explains, "In the same way you hit the brake when you're driving when you see a yellow light, when you put feelings into words, you seem to be hitting the brakes on your emotional responses."

Heidi Vermeer-Quist, a Licensed Clinical Psychologist at Pine Rest Christian Mental Health Services in Des Moines, Iowa, suggests that people can more easily hit the brakes on emotional responses and process negative feelings in any given situation by writing their reply to these questions:

- What are you feeling?
- What are you reacting to?
- How do you interpret the situation? (What is your automatic knee jerk reaction?)
- What are other response options to the situation?
- Which response option will you choose?

Coupling this journaling exercise with prayer can be a powerful approach to reaching healthier conclusions about ourselves, rather than letting emotions and feelings become the overarching reality that determine our value and worth. Adding prayer to the journaling process allows God to reveal the very truth we need to see about ourselves in a particular situation; we can ask Him to shower us with wisdom and knowledge in our effort to gain self-awareness and think through the facts.

Proverbs 18:12-14 warn us to seek the facts before we respond in haughtiness and risk crushing the human spirit. In context these verses warn us against haughtiness toward others, but they also apply to the unconscious yet insulting attitude we may have toward ourselves.

The next time you're feeling deficient in your value and

worth, take some time to journal your responses to the questions above. Then listen for God's personal message through your experience. Feelings are not facts, and that's something to celebrate!

KRISTEN CLARK

INSTILL CONFIDENCE THROUGH LETTER WRITING

In the movie, *The Letter Writer*, Bernie Diamond plays an old man whose secret is discovered by a rebellious teenage girl. His secret is that he writes personal letters of encouragement and anonymously delivers them to people who need to be uplifted; she was one such recipient. The story is about the profoundly positive impact his letters have on the readers, people who don't know the old man but who are deeply touched by (and in need of) his words.

God gives us encouragement and He wants us to encourage one another (Romans 15:5). Unfortunately, as illustrated in the movie, encouragement can be a rarity for some people. Combine that with the scarcity of the hand-written letter in this digital age and it's obvious why a simple letter of encouragement can make a lasting impression. Here are three tips for instilling confidence in others through letter writing.

1. Write from the heart. Write creatively and deliberately, and be vulnerable. Carefully consider your collection of words, thoughts, and ideas and share them in a way that reveals your spirit. Write a letter you would want to receive, a letter you would delight in, and a letter you would save for reading over and over again. Write a letter designed to inspire.

2. Write about God's love. Intimate knowledge of every details of the recipient's life is not required in order to write a letter of encouragement. However, intimate knowledge about God and His character is a must. Focus on what you know about God and write about:

- How much God loves them and forgives them.
- How God created them in His image and has a perfect plan for their lives and situations.
- How God's mercy and grace is a gift available to everyone, including them.
- How they can do all things through Him who strengthens them.
- How you also love them and are praying for them.

3. Write what you need to hear yourself. The physical act of writing punches the written words, ideas, and sentiments into our own long-term memory and causes us to focus our attention on those words, ideas, and sentiments. In writing down encouraging words for others, we are encouraged ourselves. Write what you also need to hear about your value and worth. Encourage yourself with words designed to heal your wounds, overcome your conflicts, and tackle your fears. And, write with conviction.

If you've never written a letter for the sole purpose of inspiring confidence in someone else, give it a try. Write for someone you know. Write for someone you don't. Get in the habit of telling others how much they mean and how loved they are, and tell yourself at the same time. Build confidence in others and you'll build confidence in yourself. It's amazing how that works!

GIVE YOURSELF PERMISSION

Do you find yourself waiting for the ideal moment, the perfect outcome, or some sign from above that says "go for it?" Do you worry that it's not okay to want something, or feel you don't deserve it? Are you afraid of asking for anything for yourself before everyone else's needs are met?

Many of us are taught at an early age that it's not okay to serve ourselves first at the dinner table, take the cake slice with the most icing, or get in line ahead of our invited guest. We were taught to let others go first, and some of us were punished if we didn't. After all, selfishness is rude and unattractive.

Unfortunately, our concept of selfishness can become distorted over time and result in the habit of perpetually accommodating the needs of others first, regardless of whether or not the situation warrants such generosity. By always striving to be the epitome of politeness and consideration, we may err on the side of never indulging in or nurturing ourselves.

As long as our needs and wants go unresolved, our self-image suffers. When we continuously put ourselves last on the list of priorities, we unconsciously tell ourselves (and others) that we are less important and deserving. As a coping mechanism, we may reconcile our unmet wants and needs with justification and rationalization, and continue the spiral to lower levels of confidence.

One way to correct this thinking is to give ourselves permission. In other words, we can intentionally consent to putting ourselves first when it's appropriate. We can:

- Purchase that designer necklace we've been eyeing for some time and can easily afford.
- Take an art class on Saturday mornings and improve our watercolor technique.
- Learn to crochet because it's fun, even if we're not very good at it.
- Take a trip to the Bahamas to celebrate our recent promotion.
- Repair exterior cracks in our home because it makes us feel better even if no one else cares.
- Forgive our shortcomings and accept our failures as true lessons.

Ecclesiastes reminds us that there is a time for everything, which means there is also time for satisfying and nurturing our own needs and wants. We just have to find the right balance. For example, putting our oxygen mask on first when the plane loses cabin pressure is appropriate; it is not rude, unattractive, or selfish. Why do we need to be given this permission by the attendants before each flight? I think they have some clear insight here.

While it's important to love our neighbors as we love ourselves, we also need to take care of our own wants and needs. The next time you discover that you have gone continuously unsatisfied, ask yourself why. The answer could be that you just need to give yourself permission. You'll be amazed at how good you feel about yourself when you do.

CHANGE WHAT YOU CAN, PRAY ABOUT WHAT YOU CAN'T

People who struggle with confidence often focus on the things they cannot change. Unfortunately, this focus perpetuates a common thinking disorder known as the victim mentality – blaming people, places and things, rather than taking responsibility, for one's life and circumstances.

M. Scott Peck, author of *The Road Less Traveled*, explains that it's difficult to treat this character defect. Simply put, the motto of the victim-mentality mindset is, "it's not my fault," making successful treatment challenging because "victims" do not take personal responsibility for their part in their own situation.

The Serenity Prayer, written by the American theologian Reinhold Niebuhr (1892–1971) and adopted by Alcoholics Anonymous and other twelve-step programs, is an effective tool for overcoming the victim mentality.

Serenity Prayer
God grant me the serenity
to accept the things I cannot change;
courage to change the things I can;
and wisdom to know the difference.

I use this prayer to let go of things out of my control and focus on things in my control by applying the prayer directly to my specific situation.

Here are a few examples:

"God, grant me the serenity to accept the things I cannot change, like the fact that I was recently laid-off at work. Courage to change the things I can, including my attitude and approach to looking for a new job elsewhere. And in knowing the difference, help me do my best to look for a new job rather than dwelling on the past."

"God, grant me the serenity to accept the things I cannot change, like the fact that I am the victim of identity theft. Courage to change the things I can, including my ability to file a police report, make known my situation to the credit bureaus, and complete the lengthy paperwork and process designed to protect myself. And in knowing the difference, help me focus on the blessing that the situation was identified and corrected before it got worse."

"God, grant me the serenity to accept the things I cannot change, like the fact that my husband just left me for another woman. Courage to change the things I can, including my ability to seek counseling and heal from this devastation so that I don't blame myself for the situation or unfairly judge all men. And in knowing the difference, help me use this time to heal and develop the inner strength I need to have healthy relationships with men in the future."

Using the Serenity Prayer to face challenging situations eliminates my need or desire to shift the onus of the situation to an outside influence. Rather than suggesting that I play no role in creating or improving the situation, it empowers me to change what I can about it. By not being the victim, I can focus on what I can change and affect things positively. This builds confidence.

What about those things I cannot change? Those things I leave to God, just as Philippians 4:6 reminds me to do. I turn over to Him the things I cannot affect (nor should be anxious about) so that I can play an active role in the things I can. In essence, I change what I can and pray about what I can't. I do my part and leave the rest to God.

KRISTEN CLARK

LEARN SOMETHING NEW

How we feel about ourselves plays a critical role in our overall success. Feelings of insufficiency can cause us to sell ourselves short while feelings of confidence can help us reach for the stars. Start reaching for your stars by learning something new.

One way to build inner confidence is to learn something new. By learning something new we develop and discover hidden talents and expand our knowledge and abilities. In doing so, we start to realize our capabilities and naturally begin to believe in ourselves. Thankfully, learning something new doesn't necessarily mean learning something complex or complicated. It can be as simple as learning to cook a new dish.

Here are some examples of new things to learn:

- A scientific fact, like the risk of being struck by a meteorite once every 9,300 years
- A new recipe, which could be a main dish, side dish, or dessert
- An old historic pastime like knitting or crocheting
- About a country, including somewhere you've dreamed of vacationing
- A new board game, like chess
- Good jokes and how to tell them well
- A musical instrument
- A foreign language

- A craft or skill, like building a bird houses and create a birder's paradise
- The historical and cultural impact on classic literature

Over the past six months I have learned how to drive traffic to my website, make 3D art with butterfly punches, and lower my blood pressure. I have learned about the black-bellied whistling duck, how to attract butterflies to my garden, and how sweet potatoes can help me lose weight. I have learned the art of writing an inspirational letter to a complete stranger and what to listen for when the car's brakes need replacing. But most importantly, I have learned that there's really not too much I can't do when I put my mind to it.

Develop your self-image by learning something new. Attend a continuing education class, either in person or online, and learn technology, accounting, or photography. Watch educational TV shows about nature and science. Read a book about a famous person and their legacy. Join an association or club that specializes in developing a talent you don't have but would like to. Inquire about a subject you're interested in; research it, ask questions about it, increase your curiosity of it.

Proverbs 18:15 reminds us that an intelligent heart acquires knowledge. Once you've learned something new, take some time to assess how the experience makes you feel about yourself and your abilities. Do you feel more open-minded? Do you feel a sense of creativity and innovation? Learning something new is a growth opportunity and you should notice a marked improvement in your sense of accomplishment and pride as a result.

USE YOUR CREATIVITY

There are many reasons why people lack and/or feel ill-equipped to build confidence. They may not know how to start the process. They may have never achieved anything of significance and feel the task is too daunting. They may be afraid of making mistakes or failing altogether. The good news is that building confidence can be achieved simply by using one's creativity.

Most of us are familiar with The Beginning. As the Book of Genesis outlines for us, we know that in The Beginning God created. He created the heavens and earth, light and darkness, day and night, water and land, vegetation and living creatures, and the sun, the moon, and the stars. He created all of this when the earth was formless and empty and dark. What an imagination!

Next, God created man (an equally imaginative task) and God created man in His own image and likeness. A few verses later we learn that God blessed man and said, "Be fruitful." Oh, how wonderfully made we are! We've been made to also create.

I believe God's perfect plan includes the need for creativity because He understands the value of the creative process. In fact, research over the years has shown the remarkable benefits of the creative experience. It can produce positive moods, reduce stress, and stimulate the mind, body, and spirit. It can help solve problems, nurture new ideas, and sharpen skills and abilities. But that's not all. The process of thinking up new ideas or solutions, developing those ideas into actions, and seeing the tangible outcome of those actions naturally builds confidence by providing a sense of pride and accomplishment.

Build the confidence you need by developing your creative mind. Do something each day that causes you to think more, do more, and question more. Here are some ideas to get you started:

- Create lists of ideas, solutions, and projects
- Create a new process or new way of doing something
- Create in a group and collaborate with others to build on ideas
- Create doodles and free your mind when you get stuck in a rut
- Create like a child and let go of all adult obligations stresses, strains, and worries
- Create art by learning to paint, draw, knit, write, cook, or play an instrument
- Create an experience, either for yourself or someone else
- Create a new relationship

Identify your preferred methods of creative expression and do those activities as often as you can. It might help to carve out time in your schedule just to be creative. Whether or not others see your creative work is not essential here. This exercise isn't about being the best, the most successful, or the first one done. It's about learning to listen to and trust your inner instincts and expression; it's about trying new things, improving your skills, and moving from thought to outcome. This is what builds confidence and contributes to a sense of purpose and accomplishment. Give it a try; you might surprise yourself!

SHARE YOUR EXPERTISE

Whether we realize it or not, we are each an expert in something, and identifying and sharing our expertise is a great way to build confidence. Follow these three steps to share with others your expertise, and celebrate your growing confidence in the process.

We each know more about something than someone else. In other words, there will always be someone out there who knows less than we know about a particular topic, even if we still have much to learn about it. This special skill or knowledge is what makes us experts. But we have to give away the knowledge we have in order to experience the confidence that comes with being an expert.

I happen to be an expert at writing inspirational short stories for publication. While I don't have a degree in English, I have attended writing seminars, workshops, and retreats to learn the writing craft. This is my passion and I write regularly to further develop my skills. As a result, my stories have been published in various magazines (both online and print) and in numerous compilation books, including the series published by Chicken Soup for the Soul. As a result, I am often invited to share my writing expertise with others. This is a blessing for me because sharing my knowledge with others makes me feel really good about myself. It shows me that I have something of value to offer someone else.

I suggest the following three steps to help you celebrate

your expertise and develop your personal confidence in the process.

1. Identify your special skill or knowledge. What do you know how to do really well? What do you know a whole lot about? What hobbies do you have that you love to spend time doing and have become an expert in? Expertise doesn't necessarily require knowledge in a technical area. I've met experts at creating elaborate meals on a budget, managing a profitable home daycare business, and building greenhouses for growing the most beautiful orchids. Identify what you know how to do better than most other people.

2. Share your special skill or knowledge with others. Believe it or not, there are many people who have no idea how to tackle or approach the very activity or subject you already know so much about. This is what makes you an expert. Find opportunities to share your knowledge with people interested in your subject. Teach a class for your college's continuing education program. Speak on your subject at a local library or high school. Offer a few tips to clubs, organizations, or associations. Write an article on the subject for inclusion in a magazine, newspaper, or newsletter.

3. Build upon your special skill or knowledge. Continue investing in your expertise by developing your knowledge on the subject. Take online classes, read articles, attend workshops, or join associations that focus on your area of interest. Keep learning as much as possible about your subject matter and continue to nurture your passion and knowledge of it.

1 Corinthians 3:10 reminds us of the need to be expert builders when laying down a foundation for others to build upon. In following these three steps, we identify our special skill and ensure that we remain experts as others build on our knowledge. In doing so we give back what we have received and offer something of value to others. Give it a try and see if you don't start to feel really good about yourself in the process.

SPEAK UP FOR YOURSELF

Some people are very opinionated; they seem to know exactly how they feel about everything. On the opposite side of the spectrum are those who are less dogmatic and have a tendency to defer to the ideas of others. Unfortunately, the latter behavior is often the result of fear due to a lack of confidence. Build confidence and live life to the fullest by finding and using your voice.

Most of us are familiar with the old saying, "What's good for the goose is not always good for the gander," but many of us worry that not going along with "the plan" will rustle some feathers. We fear the idea of conflict more than the idea of doing something we don't agree with or want to do. Unfortunately, peacemaking often results in compromising on something that is really important to us. This can lead to unmet expectations and deep resentments. This has certainly been true for me.

Thankfully, I have discovered three principles that I practice regularly in my effort to speak up for myself. You also might find these principles helpful:

1. Identify your truth. In order to fully know your truth about a situation you may need to take a few minutes (maybe hours or days) to assess the situation and ask yourself some questions. How do you feel about the situation? Are you comfortable with what's being expected of you? Is the situation hurtful to you – mentally, physically, emotionally, or spiritually? Do you want to participate? You may not immediately know how you feel about a particular situation. Take the time needed to fully understand your personal inner truth about what's happening.

2. Speak your truth in love and kindness. Once you have identified what you know to be true for you about the situation, voice your truth. This can be done gently. Speak your truth without shouting over other voices or stomping your foot to make a point; a soft whisper sometimes does the trick. Speak your truth without pointing fingers or placing blame. Speak openly, honestly, and candidly, but speak gently. Also, avoid the need to explain yourself. People will not always agree with or understand your position. Simply state your thoughts and resist the need to overstate them.

3. Own your truth in action. Actions speak louder than words, which is why it's important to follow up your opinion with the appropriate action. This is when you decide whether or not to go along. Avoid saying one thing and doing another. Eliminate confusion by taking the actions that align with your opinion. Don't compromise on those things that are really important to you. Spare yourself from possible resentments; if you don't want to participate, then don't participate. If you decide you want to, go for it.

I attend a number of conferences and retreats, and one year I was asked to play a part in a skit for the Saturday evening entertainment. I love skits and immediately said yes! Unfortunately, I was not comfortable with the role I was later assigned to play. While I didn't want to disappoint my friends, and realized that acting in a skit is much like pretending, I just wasn't comfortable participating in the behavior written for this particular character. I quickly became anxious about the skit and wanted desperately to back out of my commitment.

I thought about the situation for a couple of days and came to the conclusion that playing this particular character would be hurtful to me. The character's behavior was not anything I wanted to exhibit, participate in, or condone. So, I called the skit director and in a gentle and loving tone said, "You may not understand this, but I am not comfortable with this particular role and so I need to decline from the play. I am so sorry for any inconvenience this may cause you."

She was disappointed in my response, but she honored my decision and gave the part to someone else. I didn't have to make a big deal about it, either. I simply had to speak my truth in a gentle tone, and because I did I was invited to play a different role in that same skit and still contribute in a fun way. By speaking up for myself I avoided the embarrassment, guilt, and shame that often comes with not sticking to my guns, and I had a great time at the retreat with my friends.

Don't let others make decisions for you by sitting in silence. Make the conscious choice to let go of timidity and take your desired action. Speak up for yourself. You'll feel better about yourself when you do.

KRISTEN CLARK

DISCOVER AND CELEBRATE HIDDEN TALENTS

One approach to building self-esteem is discovering and celebrating hidden talents. Unfortunately, people with low self-esteem often don't know what they're truly good at. Thankfully, the things we're good at are often the very things we enjoy doing most. Follow these four steps to discover and celebrate your hidden talents and feel your self-esteem rise in the process.

Projects we enjoy doing at the office or hobbies we carve out time for during the weekends are good indicators of our talents – natural or learned. These are the activities that help us feel good about ourselves. When we experience the results of using our talents in these areas, we begin to recognize and believe more deeply in our abilities. If you want to boost your self-esteem, follow these four simple steps for discovering and using your talents.

1. Identify current interests. Make a mental note of the activities you currently enjoy and why. Ask yourself what it is specifically about these activities that inspires and satisfies you. Assess your interest and your skill. The things you already like to do are probably things you are also good at doing. Keep doing those things, and find a way to do them more often.

2. Ask others about their interests. Talk to friends, family members, and colleagues about how they discovered their passion and what they did to sharpen their skills. Perhaps you'll find that you have similar interests; if so, you can pursue those interests together. Or, temporarily borrow their interests; try their passions on for size and see how you feel about them. You might feel a little out of your comfort zone, but it may be a worthwhile experience in identifying new and exciting talents of your own. If you decide you don't like something once you've tried it, you will still have gained some great insight into yourself.

3. Research interests online. The Internet is a great way to explore new ideas and opportunities without investing significant time or money in the experience. Explore various online courses to see if anything peaks your curiosity. Check out interest groups, forums, and chat rooms and search for conversations that appeal to you. Identify why the conversation appeals to you and assess if you have the skills needed to participate. If not, take a class and learn how. If so, dive right in.

4. Take community college classes. Community college classes are an excellent way to discover talents and passions. Most classes are usually local and easily accessible. Many classes are affordable and require little additional knowledge or training. Some classes are offered frequently during the year so you can attend one at your convenience. Once you've chosen a class to attend, you'll get a good idea about the subject over the span of the course. At the end, you can decide whether or not it's right for you. If not, you can move on and try a different course until you find an interest and corresponding hidden talents that mesh well with your needs and desires.

Whatever you do, don't give up. The goal is to build self-esteem by identifying hidden talents. Make an investment in yourself by uncovering your own hidden talents and nurture those talents to your heart's content. Doing so will lead to deep fulfillment and personal satisfaction, and you might even have some fun in the process!

OVERCOME ANXIETY IN SOCIAL SITUATIONS

Most of us have experienced anxiety in social situations at one time or another. We can all feel intimidated when surrounded by too many unfamiliar faces and conversations. Unfortunately, social anxiety can be magnified for those who are unusually shy or suffer from low self-esteem. Thankfully, there is a way to overcome this intimidation.

While every social situation is different, we can choose how we respond to those situations. We can avoid social engagements because of feelings of inferiority or inadequacy, worrying about what others will think of us. Or we can look at social invitations as opportunities to develop our own interpersonal skills; with minimal effort we can become increasingly comfortable at each new meeting or event. Use these simple tips to overcome social anxiety and build confidence in the process.

1. Practice. Instead of avoiding social invitations altogether, start accepting invitations to smaller, less intimidating gatherings. Smaller gatherings can provide great opportunities to practice social skills and meet people in a less threatening environment. If the host doesn't mind, bring a friend along to help you feel more at ease. Make yourself available and practice accepting invitations and socializing with others.

2. Be your authentic self. People generally want to know the real you. Also, many of the people you meet will be equally nervous. Be your natural self and you'll help put everyone at ease. Embrace your character assets and let your inner self shine through. Remember, no one is perfect, so there's no expectation for you to be either.

3. Ask questions. People like to talk about what they know, and people know about themselves. One way to interact with strangers is to ask them questions. Ask about their background, how they like to spend their vacations, or what they like to do for fun. People will naturally open up to you and get the conversation going if you start with simple questions like these. You might also quickly discover something you have in common.

4. Breathe. Take a deep breath if you start to panic in any social situation. If necessary, excuse yourself for a few moments and find a place where you can be alone. Breathe deeply. Inhale and exhale with controlled breaths and focus on the movement of your chest. Continue breathing until you start to feel comfortable again; the flow of oxygen to the brain will relax and calm you.

5. Talk about it. Discuss your social intimidation with a trusted friend or family member. Talk about your fears and concerns, and ask for help when needed. Pray about your anxiety and ask God to remove it. Consider professional advice or assistance if your anxiety runs deep.

6. Join a club or organization. Groups and clubs are great places to practice social interaction, especially when doing so with people who share your same passions. Find a group that aligns with your hobbies and dreams and make a personal commitment to meet one new person at each meeting. You'll be amazed at how easily the conversation flows when you share something in common with someone else.

There was a time when I felt overwhelmed in social gatherings. Unfortunately, fear impeded my ability to network with others, establish new contacts, and make much needed acquaintances. With a lot of practice, I eventually overcame my social anxiety. I also discovered a deep passion for people and connecting with them on a more intimate level. As a result, I've formed some precious friendships, gifts I might have missed out on otherwise.

We are called to fellowship with one another, break bread with one another, pray with one another, and walk through life with one another. Unfortunately, this can be terribly difficult when plagued by fear and insecurities. Thankfully, fear and insecurities can be overcome. Change your attitude about social situations by embracing them as opportunities to learn and grow from and build confidence at the same time.

KRISTEN CLARK

PRACTICE THE THREE P's OF CONFIDENCE

We see examples of "making ready" everywhere. Politicians make ready for political campaigns. Athletes make ready for game night. Even people in the bible were making ready for war, burnt offerings, celebratory meals, and the coming of the King. Call it what it you like –gearing up, suiting up, saddling up – making ready requires forethought and organization prior to actual execution. These were considered ingredients for success.

Today is no different. If we want to succeed at home, work, and play, we need to "make ready". In other words, we need to plan, prepare, and practice.

- **Planning** is the process of creating a blueprint, design, or game plan for the purpose of achieving or accomplishing something. It illuminates what is needed on a given day for a successful outcome. It takes into consideration the Who, What, and When required to make something happen. For example, a Chef might plan for the opening night of a restaurant by determining the number of people expected that evening (Who), menu options and availability of specialty or seasonal food items (What), and the length of time needed to cook each dish (When). Planning enables preparation.

- **Preparation** is the process of getting ready to actually do the work. It involves thinking through what is needed to execute as planned. This may involve anticipating problems or objections, and playing out "what if" scenarios. In our example, the same Chef might prepare by acquiring specialty utensils, arranging certain herbs and spices, preparing delicate sauces in advance, or training the help needed to serve the dishes on opening night. Preparation enables execution.

- **Practice** is repeating the motions needed to ensure a successful outcome. It involves carrying out, rehearsing, or running over the steps multiple times to ensure accuracy and consistency. In our example, the same Chef might practice for Opening Night by creating the featured dishes two or three times the week prior in order to perfect the recipe. Practice enables perfection of the routine and reduces opportunities for error.

When I found myself facing a number of interviews in an effort to advance my career and income, I discovered that I did better during the interview when I planned, prepared, and practiced beforehand. I planned by scheduling the interviews far enough out that I had time to research the companies and positions I was interviewing for. I prepared by anticipating interview questions and formulating my responses to those questions. I practiced by inviting friends or colleagues to participate in mock interviews with me, asking me the very questions I prepared for. By planning, preparing, and practicing I made myself ready and executed beautifully. I increased my confidence in the process.

Zig Ziglar once said, "If you want to reach a goal, you must 'see the reaching' in your own mind before you actually arrive at your goal." See the reaching of your own personal goal by planning, preparing, and practicing, and watch your confidence soar to new heights in the process.

LEARN TO ACCEPT COMPLIMENTS

Many of us have a hard time accepting compliments. Some of us approach them cautiously, suspicious of ulterior motives, while others deflect them or point the credit elsewhere in an effort to exhibit modesty. Either way, the inability to accept compliments is a sign of low self-esteem and may show others that we don't think as highly about our actions or efforts as they do.

Improve your self-perception by following these four steps for accepting compliments with ease and grace.

1. Understand what compliments are. Compliments are simply expressions of esteem, respect, affection, or admiration; they are gestures of appreciation or approval and are often given because of something positive someone has said or done. They are polite expressions of praise. Compliments are also forms of congratulation or encouragement.

2. Identify how you naturally respond to compliments. Do you blush when a compliment is offered to you? Do you turn away or pretend you didn't hear the compliment? Do you brush it off as "nothing"? Or do you contradict the compliment with examples of your character defects in unrelated areas? Responses like these are often the result of fear – fear of appearing vain. Unfortunately, responses like these are also dangerous to our self-confidence and can perpetuate an unhealthy self-image. Awareness of our negative responses allows us to practice the opposite.

3. Start practicing new behavior. The next time you receive a compliment, practice the opposite of your normal response. Look the person giving you a complement in the eye, carefully listen to what they are complimenting you for, and smile. When they are finished giving the compliment, simply say, "Thank you." That's all there is to it. Practice this response in the mirror until you feel comfortable with it. Try it out on a trusted colleague or friend.

4. Practice giving compliments. Giving compliments is a great way to get comfortable with receiving compliments. Offer a kind and sincere word of appreciation or encouragement to someone else. Practice by giving a compliment to someone every day. Compliment someone you know. Compliment someone you don't. Keep it simple. Keep it honest. Then smile.

I once received a standing ovation for performing a song I had written. For me, that was the ultimate compliment. Afterward, people gathered around with hugs, handshakes, and more compliments. The best response I could offer was a smile and sincere "thank you." That has since become my response to all compliments.

Compliments are not a sin. They are verbal gifts of encouragement and we are called to encourage each other (1 Thessalonians 5:11). They are forms of positive reinforcement designed to build each other up. They are affirmations and offers of praise, and we can learn to fully embrace compliments in our effort to feel good about ourselves and each other.

SET CLEARLY DEFINED GOALS

Examples of goal setting can be found everywhere in the Bible. In the new testament alone we see goals of driving out demons and healing people (Luke 13:32), pleasing God (2 Corinthians 5:9), equality among people (2 Corinthians 8:14), encouraging others in heart and uniting others in love (Colossians 2:2), and loving one another (1 Timothy 1:5). Additionally, Proverbs warns us to be diligent rather than hasty in our planning and that plans fail for lack of counsel, but succeed with many advisers.

Unfortunately, most people don't actually set or define goals. Instead, they wander through life directionless and in search of purpose and significance. As a result, most people struggle to achieve their definition of success – financially, educationally, physically, artistically, socially, etc. As Benjamin Mays (minister, educator, scholar, and social activist) once said, "The tragedy of life doesn't lie in not reaching your goal. The tragedy lies in having no goal to reach."

Goal setting can have a significant impact on our overall efforts. Here are four specific reasons why:

1. Setting goals forces us to clarify what we want.
Setting goals mandates a level of specificity that we cannot ignore in our effort to be successful. In clarifying exactly what we want we are able to more easily identify how to get there and when we have arrived. By knowing what we want, we can recognize our success.

2. Setting goals motivates us to take action. You've heard the saying "out of sight, out of mind." Well, that also holds true for goals. Goals that are undefined fall off the radar screen in terms of where we invest our energy, time, and resources. When we have clearly defined goals, written down in a place that is visible, we naturally remain focused on the necessary steps to achieve those goals. They remain front and center in our mind and therefore in our decision-making process, enabling us to take the right action.

3. Setting goals provides a filter for competing opportunities. The more successful we become, the more opportunities we face, but not all opportunities will help us achieve our goals. Writing down our goals will allow us to quickly identify those opportunities that are distractions to our effort versus those that need our attention. A list of written goals then becomes a measure for us to compare new opportunities and decide which ones to pursue and which ones to pass over. It helps us be selective.

4. Setting goals enables us to see (and celebrate) progress. Being successful in anything is hard when we can't see our progress. Without celebrating our small victories we can quickly feel like we're going nowhere. By celebrating small victories, we recognize our accomplishments and measure our remaining distance to achieving our desired end result.

Early in my career I wandered aimlessly from job to job and found myself with a long resume of short-lived work experiences. I struggled to make a commitment to any one employer beyond two years, and was perceived as a flight risk by potential hiring companies.

Getting hired had become a challenge, and I had an opportunity to interview with a Fortune 50 technology company for a position I desperately wanted. Their key concern about my resume was my limited time with any one company.

Thankfully, they took a chance on me and I made a personal decision to use that company to change my resume in terms of commitment. I set myself this personal goal: to stay with that particular company for ten years before moving on.

With that goal clearly defined and top of mind, I made moves within the company (laterally and upwardly), gained invaluable work experience, and surpassed my goal by an additional six years, all of which tremendously increased my professional value internally and with other hiring companies.

Soren Keirkegaard (Danish philosopher and theologian) once said, "Our life always expresses the result of our dominant thoughts." If we want to be successful, we must define success clearly and make sure our thoughts are consumed with achieving that success. Every time we make a decision, we have the opportunity to ask ourselves whether or not that decision takes us closer to or further away from our goal. If the decision takes us closer to our goal, then we have made the right choice, but we have to identify and write down our goals before we can even decide.

MAINTAIN A CONFIDENT MINDSET FOR GREATER PERSONAL SUCCESS

Achieving success takes more than wishful thinking; it requires confident thinking. Thankfully, a positive mental inclination toward accomplishment and achievement can be developed. With these four keys, you can maintain the attitude needed to reach higher levels of personal success.

Zig Ziglar once said, "Your attitude, not your aptitude, will determine your altitude." Whether we want to build our own business, attract our perfect mate, write a best-selling book, or raise $50,000 for our favorite charity, success requires a confident attitude. Here are four keys to creating and sustaining a confident mindset for reaching the success we desire.

1. Keep company with confident people. Other people can have incredible influence over our own personal energy. That's because moods and attitudes can be contagious. A smile from a perfect stranger, for example, unexpectedly makes our day; magnify that impact a thousand times and we can begin to see the power of confident and successful friends, family and associates. When we surround ourselves with people who inspire confidence in us, believe in us, and want us to succeed, there's no room for self-doubt.

2. Repeat positive affirmations daily. Research has shown the impact positive affirmations have in helping people get through tough times. That's because repeating positive affirmations on a daily basis helps people believe what they're saying about themselves. For example, many of the most esteemed business professionals have used the same affirmation strategy to attain their success by simply repeating and believing, "I am building a powerful and profitable business." We can find the right affirmations by writing down a quick list of our doubts and insecurities. By saying the opposite, we turn these into personalized affirmations.

3. Capture negative thoughts. It's natural to have negative thoughts once in a while. However, frequent negative thoughts and emotions can derail us and prevent us from achieving our heart's desires. When we find ourselves thinking negative thoughts or having negative emotions, we can find a trigger to turn them around. Affirmations are a great way to turn the negative into a positive. Quick exercises like listening to a favorite song, taking a walk outside in the fresh air, or twenty minutes of physical exercise will also help improve our moods.

4. Maintain an attitude of gratitude. Gratitude is perhaps the single most powerful and positive tool for success. When we're grateful for all of the wonderful things and people in our lives, the challenges we face seem significantly less important and easier to deal with. Consider keeping a gratitude journal and make a practice of writing in it daily. A quick review of the blessings in our lives will help us more confidently press onward through the challenges. It's an attitude of gratitude that gives us the confidence to navigate change, overcome setbacks, and meet the needs of others more easily.

Ephesians 4:23 reminds us to make new the attitude of our minds. Success is within our reach and with the right mindset we can accomplish anything we set our sights on. By embracing these four powerful thought strategies, we can build better, more satisfying lives.

REDUCE STRESS THROUGH THE HOLIDAYS

Are you are overly cranky? Do you find it difficult to get a good night's rest? Are you on a weight roller-coaster? Do you find yourself more "on edge"? Do you feel as if the world is crashing down on top of you?

We've all experienced events that cause stress. No one is immune to this intense feeling, but when the holiday season pops up, so does the level of stress we experience. Unfortunately, stress can take its toll on our confidence.

Maintain your confidence this holiday season by using these twelve tips for keeping stress at reduced levels.

1. **Stick to a normal schedule.** Everyone needs to have a regular schedule, especially children. Try to keep up with your usual routine of eating, sleeping, resting, exercising, going to church, and of course playing. Normalcy helps reduce stress.

2. **Express your feelings.** Let others know how you are feeling. If things are bothering you, tell someone about it in a positive and constructive way. Remember, people are not good mind-readers and stress can be alleviated with honest and frequent communication.

3. **Ask for help.** If you are having difficulty shouldering responsibilities, ask someone to help. Divide up

different tasks that are on your to-do list and solicit help from friends and family. Also, don't forget to bring your prayers and petitions to God.

4. **Know your limits.** Recognize your limits and operate within them. Be gentle with yourself if you don't get everything done; show yourself some grace. Don't place high expectations on yourself, and don't make promises you can't keep. Prioritize and let the less important things go.

5. **Don't strive for "perfection."** Nobody's perfect. Do what you can and leave the rest to God. Keep in mind that you are powerless over other people, places, and things and that your best is enough.

6. **Plan realistically.** Don't underestimate the value of a good plan! Keep goals reasonable and manageable. Track your progress, adjust as needed, and celebrate your accomplishments along the way.

7. **Take a break!** Make time to relax. Treat yourself to a cup of Joe or a peaceful bite to eat at your favorite café. Practice relaxation breathing techniques. Take a short, restful nap. Treat yourself to a sweet-smelling, muscle relaxing, steamy bath. Have fun; tension is harmful.

8. **Be budget conscious.** Overspending can cause stress. Set a budget for your holiday spending and stick to it. Even Santa makes a list and checks it twice. Create a list of your gift recipients and assign a

dollar value for each gift. Use coupons. Look for sales. Spend what you have, not what you don't.

9. **Find the courage to say no.** Reduce stress by saying no to additional responsibilities. Consider saying no to requests outside of your limits, not in your plan, beyond your budget, or that interfere with taking a break. If saying no is difficult, ask God to help you find your voice.

10. **Treat yourself to a gift.** Buy yourself something this holiday season. Budget a little extra to splurge on yourself. Include yourself on your shopping list and you'll find the whole shopping experience much more fun.

11. **Use time-savers.** Paper plates, disposable silverware, plastic cups, one-use aluminum baking pans, and napkins can really cut down on your workload when throwing a friendly get-together. Use things that can be thrown out after everything is over in an effort to reduce your stress.

12. **Make time for the unexpected.** Delays are inevitable during the holiday season. Lines are longer, traffic is heavier, and life happens. Give yourself more time than expected and unplanned accidents and incidents will be easier to cope with.

PART III
AN EXPLORATION OF CONFIDENCE AS A SPIRITUAL MINDSET

CONVICTIONS AND THE ROAD TO CONFIDENCE

Alexander Hamilton once said, "He who stands for nothing will fall for anything." I love this quote because it warns us of our need for convictions – our need to believe in things with all our heart (Acts 8:37), to be compelled by an inner truth and knowledge, and to allow that inner truth and knowledge to guide us through the myriad of decisions we face each day. After all, "Strong convictions precede great actions," (Louisa May Alcott).

Do you have strong convictions? Do you believe in them with all your heart and allow them to direct your daily course? Unfortunately, many people do not. As a result they tend to:

1. Suddenly find themselves in undesirable situations asking, "How did I get here?"
2. Settle on the values of others as "good enough" and accept mediocrity.
3. Experience life as a victim, blaming people, places, and things for what happens to them.

The end result? People without deep convictions participate in and allow behavior that can interfere with their ability to reach greater heights in personal success.

Does this sound familiar? If so, **allow me to suggest a simple exercise to help you develop your personal**

internal convictions.

1. Make a list of your top five convictions. These should include those beliefs you intuitively know to be right. These should also be those beliefs you would do anything to uphold.

2. Ask yourself the following questions about each conviction:

    - Is this conviction your very own? Is this your own personal and applicable truth? (This should not be something that is "good enough" because it is learned from, handed down from, or the result of someone else's ideals or influence.)

    - Are you comfortable to stand firm on this conviction if tested? Do you know without a doubt that you would stand up for yourself because of this belief?

    - Is this conviction pleasing to God? Does it resonate with the Holy Spirit's guidance and council?

    - Does this conviction compliment your other convictions? (This conviction should not conflict or interfere with your ability to honor any of the other four.)

3. Once you have answered the questions above, reassess your list. If you answered "no" to any question in Step 2, you may need to discard that conviction and replace it with another one.

4. Over the next month, test your convictions in real-life situations. Use these top five convictions to govern your personal choices and daily decisions, and make notes about how you felt with your personal choice.

5. At the end of one month, reassess your list. Again, you may decide to discard one or two and replace them with other personal beliefs.

Here's an example of how this works for me:

1. One of my top five convictions is to protect my marriage and honor my husband.

2. This is now my very own truth. It was not my truth during my first marriage, but I have since learned the value of marriage and my role in protecting it. This is a truth I now believe with all my heart. I will stand up for my husband and honor him. This conviction aligns with the scriptures and the Holy Spirit's council, and does not conflict with any other conviction.

3. After reassessing my convictions, this one still holds true and relevant for me.

4. I tested this conviction last week when I was invited by a male colleague to go out for lunch. I felt in my heart that accepting the invitation and dining with another man alone would be dishonoring to my husband, so I invited a few other colleagues to join us. We all had great time at lunch and I was able to show my husband honor by not having lunch alone with another man. I felt really good about my decision and my ability to uphold my

vows and protect our marriage. This decision gave me more confidence in my ability to be a Godly wife.

5. At the end of one month, this conviction still resonated with my spirit deeply and remained on the list.

Do you see how this works? You might come up with more than five convictions, which is absolutely acceptable. The point is that convictions are terrific tools for achieving greater personal success. They enable us to stand up for ourselves, live authentically, and speak and act in confidence.

TWO STEPS FORWARD AND ONE GIANT STEP BACK

I had spent a lot of time studying the Bible in my effort to understand how God sees me, and I started feeling better about myself as a result. I began to embrace my value and worth in His Kingdom and my confidence naturally grew. After all, I was dearly loved; a treasured possession who was hand-picked by the Most High King.

Then suddenly, I took a turn for the worse. **As I dug deeper into the scriptures I caught a glimpse of an unexpected ugliness about myself.** I began to see how I:

- criticized and judged people harshly,
- was less than compassionate toward those who needed it most, and
- felt resentment as a result of my own unreasonable and unmet expectations.

These realizations were glaring and I felt cheated. Sound familiar?

God's desire is for us to be transformed into His likeness. As a result, He will also show us things about ourselves we'd rather not see. He will show us our weaknesses, unhealthy habits, and self-sabotaging behavior.

As John 15:2 reminds us, He will reveal our character defects so we can partner with Him while he prunes us of them. This is part of the process.

Thankfully, we have a choice in how we respond to the vulgar truth about ourselves. We can take a defeatist attitude toward what seems like a giant step back, and diminish the great work done in reversing a damaged self-image. Or, we can see through our misperceptions and rejoice in God's desire to restore us to physical, emotional, and spiritual wholeness. With His help we can unveil hidden character assets and unrecognized talents, and move forward with surer footing.

Ours is a journey of progress and not perfection which means there will be moments when we suddenly feel like we've stumbled in our confidence and self-esteem. That's normal and we can rejoice because God, the Father Almighty, will help us replace our unattractive behavior with those positive attributes that are ready to flourish and lead us to greater accomplishments.

LONELINESS AND PRACTICAL STEPS FOR OVERCOMING IT

Loneliness is a universal human emotion that visits most of us from time to time. However, loneliness is not necessarily about being alone. Instead, it is often the *perception* of being alone and feeling isolated.

Unfortunately, feelings of low self-esteem are often accompanied by feelings of loneliness. Common symptoms include:

- Thinking your problems are so unique that other people don't understand
- Feeling that other people have friends when you don't
- Feeling self-conscious in everything you do
- Feeling extremely embarrassed when you do something wrong
- Feeling disconnected and alone in a crowd
- Feeling shy and afraid to be around others
- Taking every comment or remark personally
- Believing there is something intrinsically wrong with you
- Believing no one understands how miserable you feel
- Feeling hopeless and helpless
- Feeling invisible

Thankfully, there are some practical steps to overcoming loneliness:

- Remember that feelings are not facts
- Make an effort to meet new people by joining social groups and organizations
- Spend time with loved ones and family
- Avoid songs, books, and movies that bring up feelings of loneliness
- Take care of and nurture your self – physically, mentally, emotionally, and spiritually
- Reflect on good memories and count the blessings
- Learn new skills or hobbies
- Seek medical advice for long term depression or talking privately with a counselor
- Spend time in prayer

The next time you feel overwhelmed by feelings of loneliness, remember that occasional bouts of loneliness are normal. However with the help of these practical steps, they too shall pass.

THE TRUTH ABOUT EMOTIONAL HEALING

The ability to renew our minds and build confidence often requires emotional healing from some deep injustice – caused by ourselves (as a result of our own free will and sinful nature, knowingly or not) or by someone else. Unfortunately, coping with the guilt and shame that come with the injustice and believing it was our fault can be a challenge; we may come to believe that we did something to deserve it. In many cases a divine healing is required for us to rise above the adversity and move forward with confidence.

Thankfully, divine healing is available.

Read on to learn the What and the How of Divine Healing, and take the time to review the provided scripture verses on the subject. Read what your study Bible has to say about these verses for additional clarification and insight.

Divine Healing – the "What"

When something is healed it is made sound or whole; it is mended, patched-up, cured, rehabilitated; it is brought back to its original state of purity or integrity.

I remember when my daughter's leg was put in a cast for three months. After a few x-rays, the doctor determined that she had developed stress fractures in her tibia. She was instructed to wear the cast for three months, take proper care of the cast and her leg, and follow up with him periodically. When the cast came off, her tibia was restored back to its normal state and strength. It had healed.

In the same way, a person can be emotionally healed. Julie was a dedicated employee who was laid off from work. Immediately, she fell into a deep depression and required professional counseling to recover from her feelings of loss, abandonment, inadequacy, and resentment. After a few productive sessions she was able to change her mind about herself, embrace her skills and talents, and look for another job elsewhere. She was emotionally healed from that unfortunate situation and restored to the hope that enabled her to press on toward victory – she eventually found a better job that came with a better salary.

Sometimes the injustice is more serious. Take for example cases of abuse, rape, molestation, or miscarriage. In cases like these the wound is much deeper and the best healing available is the divine healing delivered by God:

- He who forgives our sins and heals us from our diseases, including our dis-ease or uneasiness of self (Psalm 103:3);

- He who redeems our lives and crowns us with love and compassion (Psalm 103:4);

- He who restores our lives and increases our honor, comforting us once more (Psalm 71:19-21).

It is within the process of divine healing that we find peace and acceptance in our situation and become at ease with ourselves. Ultimately, we become able to face our adversities with dignity and grace, and move forward in victory. **This is good news!**

Divine Healing – The "How"

Divine healing often requires action on our part, but it is a process. This kind of divine healing rarely happens overnight. The process takes time. The process also takes an intentional effort and commitment on our part.

Not unlike the patient recovering from surgery, who is required to complete the prescribed medication, dress the wound in a certain way on a daily basis, and continue with physical therapy three times a week for the next two months, emotional healing also requires action on our part. If we choose to ignore the doctor's orders, we interfere with and slow down the healing process. Emotional healing works the same way.

Thankfully, there are a number of things we can do to assist in the healing process, and not because The Great Physician needs our help but because we grow spiritually when we take action. Here are some actions we can take:

- **We can believe** – in eternal and abundant life through the death and resurrection of Jesus Christ, who loved us and died for our sins, restoring us to righteousness (John 3:15 – 17).

- **We can read** – and digest a daily supply of the unfailing Word of God and learn about how much He loves us (Matthew 22:29, 2 Timothy 3:15-17).

- **We can share** – and fellowship with God through prayer and meditation, and with others through community (1 John 1:6-7, Acts 2:41-43).

- **We can endure suffering** – and stretch ourselves by pressing through hardship and adversity (John 15:1-3, Romans 5).

- **We can rest** – and rejuvenate (Matthew 11:28-39)

- **We can serve** – and do something helpful for someone in need (Ephesians 2:10, Matthew 10:26-28).

The point is **we can be healed**! And we can play a part in the process.

Scripture Verses on Healing

Below are just some of the areas in which emotional healing is available through divine healing. See which ones apply to you and your personal situation. Read what your study Bible has to say about these verses for additional clarification and insight.

- **Healing for Pain and Suffering – Isaiah 53:4-5**
  Expanded concepts: Fixing, renovating, repairing,

and patching up feelings of punishment, grief, and ache.

- **Healing for the Brokenhearted – Isaiah 61:1**
  Expanded concepts: Fixing, renovating, repairing, and patching up feelings of grief, sadness, depression, forlornness, heartache, melancholy, sorrow, unhappiness, and woe.

- **Freedom for Bondage – Isaiah 61:1, Luke 4:18**
  Expanded concepts: Discharging, emancipating, liberating, releasing, unbinding, unchaining, and turning loose those held in slavery, captivity, and service to pain and misery.

- **Comfort for Mourning – Isaiah 61:2**
  Expanded concepts: Assuring, consoling, reassuring, and cheering up those who are feeling sorrow and grief over loss.

- **Beauty for Ashes – Isaiah 61:3**
  Expanded concepts: Emotional healing in the form of qualities that give pleasure and exalt the mind or spirit; a particularly graceful, ornamental, or excellent quality; replacing grief, repentance, humiliation, or ruin.

- **Joy for Mourning – Isaiah 61:3**
  Expanded concepts: Feeling bliss, blessedness, gladness, and happiness instead of sorrow and grief over loss.

- **Praise for Despair – Isaiah 61:3**
  Expanded concepts: Celebrating, glorifying, and commending situations instead of feeling hopelessness or lacking in confidence about situations.

- **Double Portion and Joy for Shame and Disgrace – Isaiah 61:7**
  Expanded concepts: Feeling eternal, endless, permanent, undying, and unending joy and double portions in blessings in place of regret, remorse, guilt, humiliation, and dishonor.

- **Sight for Blindness – Luke 4:18**
  Expanded concepts: Vision, rational discrimination, guidance, direction, awareness, and consciousness to those whose judgment is restricted, clouded, and lacking in discernment.

- **Freedom for Condemnation – Romans 8:1-2**
  Expanded concepts: Freedom from blame, rebuke, reprimand, reproach.

- **Dancing for Wailing – Psalm 30:11-12**
  Expanded concepts: Gaiety, bliss, delight, and gladness in place of lamenting, complaining, grumbling, moaning, and whining.

- **Justice for the Injured – Isaiah 30:18-19**
  Expanded concepts: Righteousness, fairness, equity, and sympathy for those who have been wronged.

HEALING FROM ABUSE: REGAINING SELF VALUE AND WORTH IN THE WAKE OF GOD'S LOVE

Abuse of any kind is a crime. Sexual abuse, physical abuse, mental abuse – no one deserves to suffer from this kind of treatment or behavior. Most people don't bring this cruelty upon themselves. Yet, so many victims feel responsible. Thankfully, victims can heal from this abuse by walking in the wake of God's Love.

Have you ever experienced the wake of something powerful? Perhaps you've heard stories of those who have experienced the wake of floods, tornadoes, earthquakes, or Poseidon and emerged stronger, wiser, and enlightened. The wake is the track or path left as a result of some experience. It is the result or consequence of some profound event.

Survivors of abuse often experience an array of overwhelming feelings. They may feel fear, guilt, and shame. They may experience intense anxiety, stress, or depression. Finally, they may suffer from significant self-doubt, inferiority, insignificance, and worthlessness.

Thankfully, healing and recovery can be found in what I call the WAKE of God's Love. Use the following acronym to experience the wake of God's love in an effort to recover from the tragedy and devastation of abuse and let the healing begin.

W: Worth. Our value and belief in self can be restored by understanding how much value and worth God places on us. Whether we think ourselves worthy or not, He deems us worthy and healing begins by focusing on His perspective. After all, considering the damage that abuse does to our own ego and psyche, our perception is likely distorted. By seeing ourselves as He sees us, we can correct our self-image. Remember, we have been purchased for a high price; He gave His one and only Son for us. We are his treasured possession. We are beautiful and His perfect bride. We have been created for His glory and we are a good and perfect gift. We are dearly loved and valuable to Him. He sees our beauty and our potential. We can heal by focusing on what He sees.

A: Adoration. Healing can continue when we start to receive God's perfect love. The truth is He knows everything about us, including every flaw and imperfection, and still he loves and accepts us as we are. He created us and he wants to protect us. As a result, we will not perish; we are not condemned. Rather, we are forgiven and thus the beneficiaries of abundant and eternal life. We are hand-picked and restored to friendship with Him. He wants a relationship with us and so he continuously pursues our love and our hearts. We have been crowned with love and compassion. By embracing His love for us we can begin to love ourselves again.

K: Kindness. We can begin to acknowledge and receive God's good gifts and blessings by understanding His kindness toward us. Because God loves us so much, He extends to us a special favor or grace. We are heirs to His throne. He loves us and He has blessings in store for us. He showers us with grace, not because we deserve it or have earned it, but because He loves us and we need it. By receiving His Kindness, we participate in the transformation from Victim to Royalty; we no longer need to cling to feelings of unworthiness because we can appreciate the blessings that are set aside for children of a King.

E: Empowerment. We can emerge victorious by understanding how God equips us for success. With His help, we become increasingly joyful, peaceful, forbearing, kind, good, faithful, gentle, and self-controlled. We also become more loving, of others and of ourselves. These are the very attributes that allow us to mend, grow, heal, and restore our souls from the damage done. We are holy and blameless. We are redeemed and restored to righteousness, and we can do all things through Him who strengthens us. In essence, we are empowered for greater success through His Hand, His Guidance, and His Strength.

We are valued and adored by the Most High King. As a result, He shows us special kindness and empowers us for great things. This is the divine and profound experience of His Love. This is the result and lasting effect of knowing God, and it is by walking in this WAKE that we overcome feelings of inferiority, insignificance, and worthlessness. This is how we develop confidence in ourselves, rise above devastating ordeals, and heal.

KRISTEN CLARK

SIX WAYS TO GROW SPIRITUALLY, CONNECT WITH GOD, AND INCREASE CONFIDENCE

Our ability to grow spiritually requires an intentional and intimate relationship with God. In connecting with Him on a deeper level, we learn to trust Him to do what we cannot do ourselves. In essence, we increase our confidence – in Him and in us. Use the suggested approaches below to develop your faith and increase your confidence in God.

Faith is the key to spiritual growth and requires a deep and personal connection with God. He wants to be the head of our hearts, king of our souls, and guide to our spirits. By allowing Him free reign in these areas we create an opportunity for lasting intimacy with the Creator. From intimacy comes confidence – in Him and in us. Here are six ways I increase my faith and confidence. You might also find them helpful.

1. Pray. Reach out to God through prayer and surrender to him everything that makes you anxious and worried; let go of those things you are powerless over and let God meet your needs with His grand and divine solutions. Present to Him your heart-felt concerns and listen for His wisdom and guidance. Don't forget to praise Him in the process, showing your gratitude and thanksgiving for all He has done for you. Connect with God through prayer and feel the unexplainable peace that will protect your heart and mind through all situations.

2. Read the scriptures. The scriptures are the foundation for our success. They direct our paths and encourage our efforts. They offer life lessons and suggest compelling principles to live by. Make time every day to read the scriptures in your effort to understand God's plan for you and apply His teachings to your life. Read a Study Bible for additional context and clarity, and any other scriptures referenced. Let God's Word be your compass.

3. Fellowship with God and others. Keep company with God and those who also want to grow spiritually. Learn from the experience, strength, and hope of those who have gone before you. Listen to and apply their wisdom and truth to your own life circumstances. Pray together. Dine together. Praise God together. Read the Bible together. This is how we hold each other accountable and invite help where we need it most.

4. Embrace suffering and adversity. Life happens and nowhere does it say that life with God makes us immune to or free from trials and tribulations. Stretch yourself by pressing through hardship and adversity. Experience suffering in all aspects. It is through difficulties that we develop the talents and skills God will use later. It is through hard times that we grow – in faith, confidence, and strength. Experience the pain and celebrate the progress.

5. Rest and rejuvenate. We often make things harder because we don't take the time to nurture and care for ourselves. We are not Super Heroes. We are human beings with limitations. It is critical that we recognize our limits and tend to our needs in order for us to be our best, reach our highest potential, fulfill our noble purpose, and be the very person God created us to be. Make time for quiet and peace, and listen for God's personal message for you. Be still and know that He is God.

6. Participate in service work. Find opportunities to help others. Serve in ministry at your church. Serve in community at your local library or hospital. Volunteer your time and talents to help someone else. When we help others we get out of self and become an instrument God can use. Be a good steward of opportunities for assistance; don't hesitate when the need arises and serve with a heart of willingness and humility.

Spiritual growth takes time. Not unlike other relationships, developing an intimate and personal relationship with God requires an effort on our part. It requires us to be willing, present, and vulnerable. When we offer ourselves in this regard, and follow the steps outlined above, we mature spiritually and connect with God on deeper levels. In essence, we grow in confidence – in Him and in ourselves.

FEAR-CONQUERING SCRIPTURE

Psychologists agree that fear and anxiety are the foundation of low self-esteem and people with low self-esteem suffer from specific kinds of fear including:

- Fear of Inadequacy
- Fear of Loss
- Fear of Failure
- Fear of Abandonment
- Fear of Hardship, Depression, or Devastation

While fear may be natural for many of us, we have a choice in how we respond to it. We can take a defeatist attitude toward our situations and buckle beneath the weight of our worries. Or, we can rejoice in God's desire to restore us to physical, emotional, and spiritual wholeness by embracing His promises, as outlined in the scriptures. Let's look at the scripture for each category of fear listed above.

Fear of inadequacy (being deficient, insufficient, or undersupplied; lacking in or being short in):

- John 15:5 – He is the vine; remain in Him and you will bear much fruit.
- Philippians 4:13 – You can do all things through him who strengthens you.

- 2 Corinthians 12:9-10 – His grace is sufficient for his power is made perfect in weakness; when I am weak, then I am strong.
- Isaiah 64:8 – We are the clay and the work of His hand.
- Jeremiah 29:11 – He has plans to help you be strong and flourish, plans to give you hope and a future.

Fear of loss (loss of things, relationships, dreams, opportunities) or of not having enough (food, money, clothes, shelter):

- Proverbs 3:5-6 – Trust in the Lord and He will make your paths straight.
- Matthew 6:25-33 – Do not worry about food or clothing, God will provide for you the same way He provides for the birds of the air and you are more valuable than they. Seek first His Kingdom and He will provide for your needs.
- 2 Corinthians 9:8 – God blesses you so that you will have all you need.
- Psalm 55:22 – Give your burdens over to God and he will sustain you (nourish and nurture you).
- Isaiah 58:11 – He will satisfy your needs and provide when you are in need of quenching and strength.
- Psalm 33:18-19 – Keep your eyes on Him and He will deliver you from death and keep you alive in famine.

Fear of failure (lacking in accomplishments, achievements, and success):

- 1 Chronicles 22:13 – Follow God's commands and He will give you success; do not be afraid.
- 2 Chronicles 20:20 – Have faith in God and he will bring you success.
- Proverbs 2:6-8 – He plans success for the decent and honorable; he guards the course and protects the way of his faithful ones.
- 2 Chronicles 26:5 – He sought the Lord, and God gave him success.
- Deuteronomy 20:3-5 – Do not be afraid, for God goes with you to give you victory.
- Psalm 20:6 – The Lord gives victory to His chosen people.
- Psalm 149:4 – God crowns the humble with victory.
- 1 John 5:3-5 – Everyone who believes in Jesus Christ overcomes the world and has victory.

Fear of abandonment (being deserted, left behind, withdrawn and pulled away from):

- Joshua 1:9 – Be strong and courageous, for God is with you wherever you go.
- Genesis 26:24 – I am the God of Abraham; do not fear, for I am with you.

- 2 Corinthians 4:8-10 – We are hard pressed on every side, but not abandoned.
- Deuteronomy 31:6-7 – Do not be afraid, He will never leave you nor forsake you.
- Joshua 1:5 – No one can stand against you because I will be with you; I will never leave you nor forsake you.
- Psalm 9:10 – God has never forsaken those who seek Him.
- Isaiah 42:16 - God will lead the blind, guiding them through rough places, and never forsaking them.
- Hebrews 13:5 – Be content because God has said, "Never will I leave you; never will I forsake you."

Fear of hardship, depression, or devastation (being overwhelmed and helpless; suffering and difficulty):

- Psalm 23:4 – I fear no evil for you are with me, your rod and staff comfort me.
- Isaiah 49:13 – The Lord comforts His people and has compassion on those in agony.
- Isaiah 66:12-13 – The Lord will bring peace; as a mother comforts a child, so will He comfort you.
- Jeremiah 31:13 – He turns mourning into gladness; He gives comfort and joy in place of sorrow.
- Matthew 5:3-4 – Blessed are the poor in spirit, those who mourn, for they will be comforted.

- 2 Corinthians 1:3-5 – God is the Father of compassion and comforts us in all our troubles.

In an effort to build self esteem, we must conquer fear. Thankfully, this can be done by understanding who we are and Whose we are.

Read the provided scripture verses for each type of fear listed above. Read these verses in your study Bible. Pray for God's wisdom and discernment about their personal meaning to you. Meditate on the truth about God's provision for you, believe, and rejoice!

KRISTEN CLARK

ESTEEM-BUILDING SCRIPTURE

In an effort to build self-esteem and confidence, it helps to understand who we are and Whose we are. Below are thirty scripture verses that explain your value and worth in His Kingdom. Read these verses in your study Bible, pray for God's wisdom and discernment about their personal meaning to you, meditate on the truth about how God sees you, and rejoice! You are wonderfully and remarkably made!

- 1 Chronicles 16:34 - His love endures forever.

- 1 Corinthians 6:20 - You have been purchased for a price.

- 1 John 4:9 – 10 – He loves you and sent His son to die for you.

- 2 Corinthians 5:17 – You are a new creation.

- 2 Corinthians 5:20 – You are His ambassador.

- 2 Corinthians 3:18 – You are being transformed into his likeness.

- 2 Corinthians 12:9-10 – His grace is sufficient; His power is made perfect in your weakness.

- 2 Thessalonians 2:13 – You are chosen and hand-picked by Him.

- Colossians 3:12 - You are dearly loved.

- Deuteronomy 26:18 – You are his treasured possession.

- Deuteronomy 31:6 – He will never leave you.

- Ecclesiastes 3:11 - You are beautiful.

- Ephesians 1:4-7 – You are holy and blameless; you are the King's daughter; redeemed and restored to righteousness.

- Genesis 1:27 – You have been created in His image.

- Hebrews 8:12 – You are forgiven.

- Hosea 2:19 – You are His perfect bride.

- Isaiah 64:8 – You are the work of His Hand.

- Isaiah 43:6-7 – You have been created for His glory.

- James 1:17 – You are a good and perfect gift.

- Jeremiah 29:11 – He has a plan to prosper you, not to harm you.

- John 1:12 - You are His beloved.

- John 1:16 – He has blessings in store for you.

- Luke 12:7 – You are valuable to Him.

- Philippians 4:13 – You can do all things through His strength.

- Psalm 139:5 – You are blessed by His Hand.

- Psalm 139:10 – His Hand will guide you; His strength will support you.

- Psalm 139:14 – You are so wonderfully made.

- Romans 8:17 - You are heir to His Throne.

- Romans 8:38-39 – He will let nothing separate you from His love.

- Psalm 103:4 – You have been crowned with love and compassion.

KRISTEN CLARK

BIBLE STUDY TIPS

As human beings, we don't always see things accurately. We often have misperceptions, which psychologists attribute to seeing things through distorted lenses. Our lenses become distorted by our wants, needs, prejudices, experiences, education, and memories.

Unfortunately, because of our distorted lenses, our brain can take over our thoughts, attack our self-worth, and question our abilities. This happens when deceptive brain messages intrude into our psyche; left to its own devices, our brain can cause us to believe things that are not true.

I want to see the truth. More specifically, I want to see God's truth and there is nothing in the Bible that claims or suggests that God has distorted lenses. In fact, He does not. He is perfect, and I want to see what He sees. I want to see His crystal clear, accurate, certifiable truth.

So, I turn to the Bible. I turn to the Bible because I believe; I believe the Bible is the infallible Word of God. I believe it is entirely truthful, not only for me but for you as well.

As you review the scriptures presented in this book to search for God's truth, you may find the following tips helpful. These suggestions will prepare you for a breakthrough in your effort to become a Woman of Worth.

1. **Study with a Dictionary.** One thing I've learned over the years is that I don't know the correct definition of every single word in the English language. Do you? That's why it's helpful to use a dictionary, either in printed format or online. Use a dictionary to look up the key words in the verses you are studying to make sure you interpret the scriptures accurately. Don't forget to read the synonyms, which are words or expressions that have the same or nearly the same meaning as the word looked up.

2. **Use a study Bible.** Make sure you have a study Bible as you study the scriptures. A study Bible includes notes and references to help readers understand the context of the scriptures and their meaning. The notes and references are not necessarily divinely inspired, although I find them extremely helpful. In fact, I like to use two study Bibles when interpreting the scriptures.

3. **Use two or three different translations of the Bible.** Use different translations when studying select verses in an effort to see how different translators have interpreted the original language. You may find that one translation speaks to you differently than another. Also, reading multiple translations may give you greater insight into how a verse applies to you specifically. Popular versions include New International Version (NIV), New King James Version (NKJV), and New American Standard Bible (NASB).

4. **Pray for understanding and revelation.** Before reading the scriptures, ask God to enlighten you with

divine understanding and clarity about the personal message He has for you. Ask Him to shower you with wisdom, discernment, and conviction as you read specific verses and internalize them for yourself.

5. **Keep a journal.** Keep a journal while studying the Bible and capture in writing your personal thoughts, key insights, and revelations. Reviewing your entries every few days may increase your clarity and wisdom regarding what God's word says to you and about you.

6. **Make it a habit.** Psychiatrists and psychologists agree it takes an average of 21 days to break a habit or start a new one, and that habits determine 95% of thoughts, feelings, and actions. Did you also know that habits are the result of repeated controlled actions? Get in the habit of studying God's Word daily by making it a priority to read and study your Bible every day over the next 21 days.

7. **Get a study buddy.** Finding someone to study with does two things: it makes you accountable (responsible) for keeping the commitment you made to study God's Word, and it provides you with someone to reason things out and discuss key insights and personal revelations as a result of reading the scriptures. An ideal study buddy will respect confidentiality, pass no judgment, set clear boundaries, show up on time to scheduled sessions, stay on target, and invite follow up for progress.

Being accountable and sharing your thoughts with another human being can challenge or confirm your interpretation of the scripture, both of which can lead to increased clarity about God's personal message for you. Also, this accountability and exchange of key insights can be done in person (face to face), over the phone, or online. Either way, the sharing of ideas and accountability will enable you to be more successful in your Bible study efforts.

8. **Study where it's comfortable.** Find a location that's comfortable for studying and take into consideration what you need in terms of lighting, seating, table-top space, and atmosphere. Create an environment that accommodates your personal learning style and promotes prayer and meditation. Try out a few different locations until you find one that works best for you. Other things to consider include sounds, smells, and sights. Do these factors increase or decrease your ability to focus and concentrate on God's personal message for you?

WOMAN OF WORTH AFFIRMATION

I know who I am and I am a woman of worth.
I can see how God sees me and I am valuable.
I am a daughter of the Most High King.
I am created in His image.
I am the work of His Hand.
He knows everything about me and I trust Him
to complete this good work in me.
I am dearly loved, His treasured possession,
and set apart for a noble purpose.
I am an heir to His Throne
with a divine destiny to fulfill.
By His Grace, I pledge to be
all He wants me to be, that I might be a good
representation of the One who created me.
I am special, unique, and important -
to God and those He puts in my path.
I can do all things
through Him who strengthens me.
He has a plan for me.
Therefore, I will jealously guard my mind
from anything that would defile this knowledge,
and I will glorify Jesus Christ.

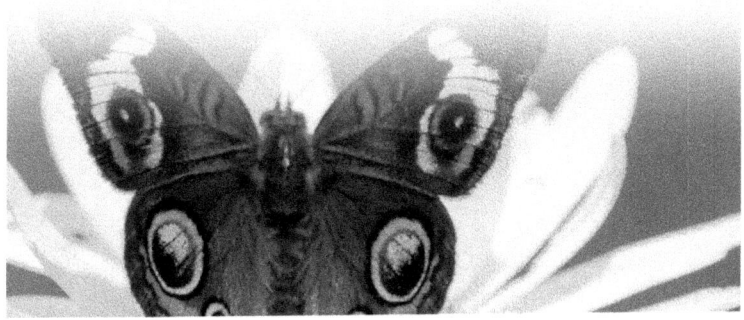

KRISTEN CLARK

HOW YOU CAN HELP

Did you enjoy this book? Please help spread the word!

One great way is to post a link to Facebook and invite your friends to have a look. Here's a simple message you can copy and paste:

When we believe we can, we do – even when it seems all odds are against us. No one knows this better than Kristen Clark, author of this exciting new book! Check it out at http://tinyurl.com/mc4nq23. It received 5 Stars from Readers Favorite.

Here are some other easy ways to help:

- Tell your colleagues and friends about this book. Talk it up over coffee, during phone conversations, at association gatherings, etc.
- "Like" Kristen's FaceBook page: Kristen Clark - Coach.
- Order a copy of the book for a friend.
- Post a review of Becoming a Woman of Worth on Amazon.
- Use this book as a book study with a small group.
- Recommend me to speak on this topic for an upcoming keynote, fund-raiser, or retreat.

Thanks so much for your support!

ABOUT THE AUTHOR

ABOUT THE AUTHOR

I am a creature of habit; I love routines. And one routine I have is the morning practice of standing in front of our bathroom mirror to get ready for the day. I brush my teeth in front of the mirror. I style my hair in front of the mirror. I put on my makeup in front of the mirror. I get dressed in front of the mirror. I put on my jewelry and finishing touches in front of the mirror. Finally, I check myself in the mirror before I head out to greet the world.

Some days I really like what I see in the mirror. Some days I'm not all that thrilled with what I see, but I consider this progress because there was a time in my life when a day didn't go by that I didn't like what I saw in the mirror.

During much of my life, when I looked in the mirror I saw inadequacy. I thought I wasn't good enough, smart enough, pretty enough, funny enough… fill in the blank; I wasn't enough of it! I compared myself to other people and always believed I didn't measure up. I often had difficulty finding my own self-worth, and I let other people define my value. I suffered from low self-esteem and my greatest fear was that I would never amount to anything worthwhile, that I held no significant value.

I was afraid no one would want me or love me just as I was. My parents didn't instill this in me; it was simply what I chose to see. At the end of the day, I didn't like my reflection, and my actions and my words showed that

I didn't like my reflection.

Unfortunately, I suffered from misperception of self. I failed to see the truth and reality of who I was. Instead, I saw myself through distorted lenses. One day, a woman at church said to me, "Kristen, I wish you could learn to see yourself as God sees you because you are amazing."

I didn't know what that meant – to see myself as God sees me – but I had lived in enough pain for so long that I wanted to find out. So, I embarked on a journey and began the process of reprogramming my brain to align with what God's Word says about who I am, in Him, and I began to understand my noble purpose. As a result, I want to share my experience, strength, and hope in an effort to help other women shed their perception of self and become Women of Worth.

When not speaking or writing on *this* subject, I speak and write on living with gratitude and writing for publication. My articles have appeared in numerous online journals and magazines, while my inspirational short stories have been published in several volumes of Chicken Soup for the Soul.

I also have over twenty years experience working in small business and corporate America, and a wealth of practical business knowledge. I have successfully held positions in Sales, Management, Strategy & Planning, Marketing, and Executive Communication.

I live in Houston with my darling husband, Lawrence, who is a writer, speaker, musician, and educator.

Finally, I LOVE butterflies. Among other things, butterflies symbolize transformation, renewal, and rebirth. They symbolize the miracle of a real metamorphosis and the possibility of such a miracle within each and every one of us. As a result, thanks to your purchase of this book, a portion of the proceeds have been donated to the National Butterfly Center to expand the education, conservation, and scientific research of butterflies.

For more information about my other speaking topics, including The Gratitude Factor for Increased Personal Success, Confidence for Greater Personal Success, Inspirational Writing for Those Wanting to Share Their Message, and The Five C's to Success, or to hire me to speak at your church, company, or organization, visit www.kristenclark.org, email Kristen@kristenclark.org. I would love to talk to you about my availability and fees.

Cheers!

Kristen Clark

www.HisSideoftheLookingGlass.com
www.BecomingaWomanofWorth.com
www.LivingwithGratitude.com
www.KristenClark.org
www.AllThingsButterflies.com

INCREASE YOUR SELF ESTEEM IN JUST 21 DAYS

Psychiatrists and psychologists agree it takes an average of 21 days to break a habit or start a new one, and that habits determine 95% of thoughts, feelings, and actions. Did you also know that habits are the result of repeated controlled actions, and that poor habits interfere with success, cause you to sell yourself short, and may result in negative consequences?

With my program, 21 Day Journey to Seeing Yourself as God Sees You, you will shed perception of self and develop a realistic mindset about your value and worth in God's Kingdom. And, you will gain the confidence you need to stop selling yourself short and start accomplishing more.

Meet Julie

Julie was 17, overweight, painfully shy, and depressed. In spite of her many talents, she suffered from low self-esteem. She thought she wasn't good enough, smart enough, talented enough, aggressive enough…fill in the blank, and she thought she wasn't enough.

I invited Julie to spend 21 days with me reading scripture, praying, meditating, and learning about how she is dearly loved, beautiful and blameless, perfectly made, and crowned with God's love and compassion. Shortly after our 21 days together, Julie decided her job as a night-time security guard simply wasn't her heart's desire; she deeply wanted to be a fashion designer.

Motivated toward something more, and with a new found confidence, she applied to a fashion design school in California (an opportunity she never thought possible before). She's now in her second year and well on her way to reaching her highest potential.

This unique and transformational program:

- Is a **flexible and easy-to-use online program**… offering you the freedom to participate at your **convenience** each day, without leaving your home.

- Includes **program instructions emailed each day** for each activity… keeping you on track with **simple reminders and tips for success.**

- Incorporates **30 scripture verses** about your value and worth… helping you build **confidence** and stop selling yourself short.

- Encourages daily **prayer and meditation**… allowing you to discover new **insights and truths** through a deep **spiritual awakening.**

- Includes **three recordings on inspirational topics**… allowing you to **learn from** scripture and my experience, strength, and hope as a result of going through this program.

- Is a **21 day** program… enabling you to develop and continue **the habit of a positive mindset.**

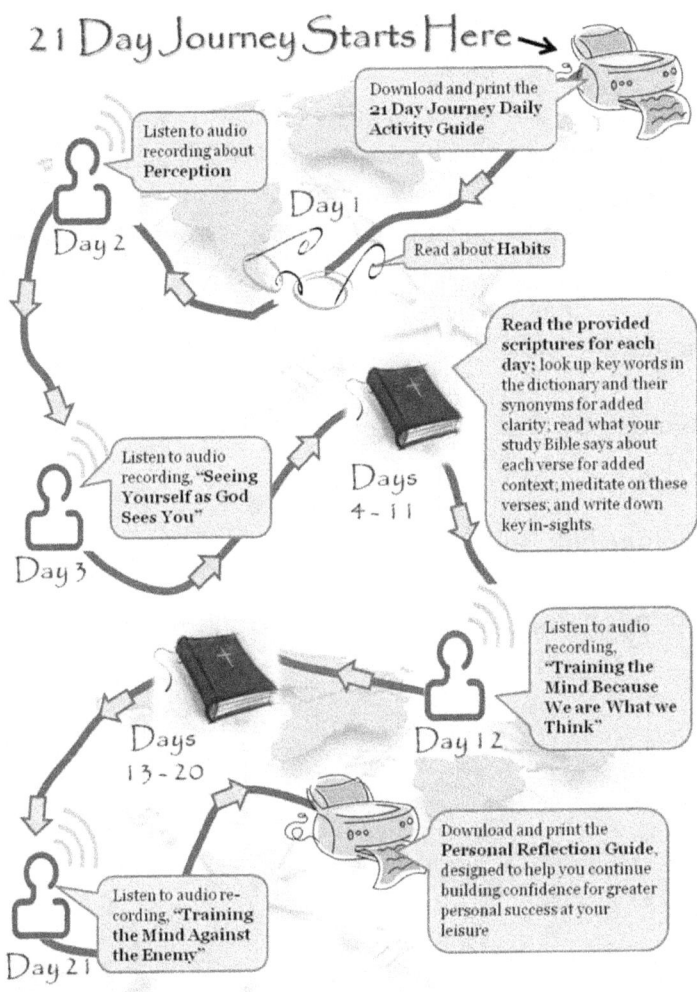

And, the program comes with this BONUS! Seven days of reflections and thought-provoking questions designed to help you continue building confidence for greater personal success! Use this downloadable Personal Reflection Guide to compliment your 21 Day Journey, or to extend your journey another seven days.

The Choice is Yours. The Time is Now.

You can keep doing what you've always done, and keep getting what you've always gotten. OR, you can make an investment in yourself and the future you've always wanted. Treat yourself to something special, something life-changing. You deserve nothing less. Experience it for yourself and transform your life in ways you never thought possible.

Sign up now and begin to embrace the greatness within you.

Visit the link below to register today.

http://hissideofthelookingglass.com/introductory-offer/

www.ingramcontent.com/pod-product-compliance
Lightning Source LLC
LaVergne TN
LVHW021343080426
835508LV00020B/2101